...And Then I Met God

by

Wanda M. Lawson

This book is a work of fiction. Places, events, and situations in this story are purely fictional. Any resemblance to actual persons, living or dead, is coincidental.

ISBN: 1-4033-2818-8 (ebook)
ISBN: 1-4033-2819-6 (Paperback)

This book is printed on acid free paper.

1stBooks - rev. 11/01/02

Acknowledgments:

All Poems by Wanda M. Lawson © 1997, 1998, 1999, 2000

Scripture quotations are from the New King James Version, © 1979, 1980, 1982 Thomas Nelson, Inc.

"On Summers Passing" – © Copyright 1998 The National
   Library of Poetry as a compilation
"Outstanding Poets of 1998" – © Copyright 1998
   The National Library of Poetry as a compilation
"America at the Millennium: The Best Poems and Poets of
   the 20th Century" – © Copyright 2000 The National
   Library of Poetry as a compilation

Dedication

This book is dedicated to the Most High, Father God, who pulled me out of Egypt and delivered me from the hand of Pharaoh.

To my mother, Claudine Lawson and my son Dwayne Lawson-Brown, who didn't always understand but never discouraged me;

To the man who saw me at my weakest and stood by me anyway, E. L. Barnes;

My friend, Stacey Miles: we have watched each other grow, encouraged each other and in a crowd of many been the only two to stand for God.

My church, Emmanuel Baptist Church, God is indeed with us;

To Pastor Clinton W. Austin: You have watched me grow, let me make mistakes and encouraged me to stand.

My fellow prayer warriors, Children of the Living God: our morning prayers have been heard, many strongholds have been broken, victory is ours.

Always remember you are Children of God. Never let the devil defeat you. He is under our feet. We are above and not beneath, the lender and not the borrower, blessed going out, and blessed coming in, we have high favor with God. We are His children! He will never leave us.

I Love You more than you will ever know. Thank you!!!!!!!!

Contents

About the Book

As with a mirror and opened door let me take you through the journey of how this book began...

I woke up that morning the same way I always do. It was to me an ordinary day. I got up and went to work. It was early September, late summer. The year 1997 and the days were getting cooler. At work someone said they had heard that they were having prayer across the street in the garage and asked me if I wanted to go. I said yes. I wasn't really looking for anything special. I just wanted to go and pray. There were a lot of people there. Saints, children of God and me. Like I stated before I wasn't looking for anything special, just to pray. As I closed my eyes I asked God "Can you do anything with me?" He said, "Yes". Then I felt these enormous arms around me and I felt peace. This was the first time as an adult I can remember ever having peace. It is a good thing to be with God. Not long after that experience the poem <u>Come Unto Me</u> was born.

This book is in two sections. Section I is the poetry. The scripture references proceeding the title of the corresponding poem in Section II.

Ultimately, we must pray to God for deliverance from our strongholds (problems/sins) and let Him bring us out. These scriptures, as well as other, have inspired me and helped me to grow, so I'm passing them on to you.

My fellow warriors: we are few, we are blessed, we are highly favored, and we are children of God.

May God bless and continue to keep you.

Your sister in Christ

Wanda

Introduction

My life was in turmoil,
I saw no change.
It was time for rearranging,
my life had to change.
I was falling and falling,
I could not stop.
I cried out for help.
And then I met God.
He saved me from this world.
He saved me from myself.
When I cried out,
He came to help.
My life needed rearranging,
my life had to change.
I was falling and falling
I could not stop.
I cried out for help.
And then I met God.
My life has been renewed.

Wanda M. Lawson

Section I

The Poetry

Wanda M. Lawson

LOOK AT WHAT WE'VE DONE TO WHAT GOD GAVE US

God gave us a mouth
so we could talk,
but all we do is
scream and squawk.
God gave us a smile
to last awhile,
but all we do is put
down someone's child.
God gave us freedom
to do as we please,
would you look at
what you've done
to me?
God gave us kindness
to be sweet,
but all we do is
cheat, cheat, cheat!
God sent us bread
and said to share,
but we don't spread
it anywhere.
The thanks we give
God for all He's done,
is war and pain that
starts with a gun.

UNTITLED

It is not for us to
decide who is right
and who is wrong.
That isn't up to us,
it's up to God.
We do not have the
right to be prejudice
against anyone.
However, we do
have the right to
be different.
That's what makes
us individuals,
special, it makes
us human.
That's what makes
us mankind.
A step above
the animals.
And isn't that what
God intended?

Unto The Lord

I lift my hands
unto the Lord,
for He has given
me peace.

I bow my head
unto the Lord,
for the things
He's given me.

I lift my eyes
unto the Lord,
for He has
done great
things for me.

He feeds me,
protects me
and guides me
all my days.

He hides me
and shields me
from unknown
dangers always.

Wanda M. Lawson

I lift my hands
unto the Lord,
for He has given
me peace.

I bow my head
unto the Lord,
for the things
He's given me.

I lift my eyes
unto the Lord,
for He's done
great things
for me.

I give my soul
unto the Lord,
for He has set
me free.

COME UNTO ME

One day Jesus came to me
and told me my every deed.
And then to me Jesus said:
"My child I still love thee."
Come unto me and live a
life more precious than
silver or gold.
Come unto me and I will
show you miracles never told.
Come unto me and I will
show you a future full
and bright.
Come unto me and I will
give you everlasting life.

Wanda M. Lawson

HOW PRECIOUS I MUST BE

Yet, before I was born Jesus
cared enough for me to die.
How precious I must be to Him.
Greater than all the gold and
precious jewels.
Oh, how Jesus must love me.
How glorious I must have looked
to Him as He hung there and died.
He looked past all of my
transgressions and saw what
I was going to be:
victorious, blessed and
saved by His grace.
How precious I must be to Jesus
for He laid down His life for me.

CHILDREN OF THE LIVING GOD

Sometimes we will have problems,
but don't despair.
We are in this world,
but we are not of it.
God hears our prayers,
He sees us when we cry,
He dries all our tears,
For He has always loved us.

We may be beaten,
but we will not die.
We may lose some battles,
but the war is won.
Persecuted, but not defeated.
Hurt, but not destroyed.
In your trials, count it all joy.
For by Jesus' blood,
we have been redeemed.
We have the victory!
For we are
CHILDREN OF THE LIVING GOD!
Our war is already won.

Wanda M. Lawson

How I Love Thee

Oh God, how I love thee,
the world will never know.
Just looking at how you've
blessed me,
sure has blessed my soul.
Oh Lord, how I love thee,
mere words can not compare.
No word has been formed that
can show you how much I care.
Oh Lord, how I love thee,
the world will never know.
Just looking at how thou hast
blessed me,
sure has blessed my soul.

Why Are We Here?

We're not here to judge the sinner,
For we all have sinned.
We're not here because we're perfect,
We all have flaws.
We're not here because we're always right,
Remember, we're not perfect.
We're not here to hurt each other,
No one wants to be hurt.
We're not here to hate each other,
Everybody wants to be loved.

So why are we here, I wondered,
And this is what I found:

We're here to lift our brothers up,
To let them know God cares.
We're here to teach our sisters
it's ok to praise God anywhere.
We're here to teach our children
God loves you and we do to.
We're here to teach each other
God cares for me and for you.
We're here to hold each other up,
For when one falls, so do we all.

We're here to do what Jesus said
for those who are not in the light:

We're here to open their eyes,
and turn them from darkness to light,
and from the power of Satan unto God,
that they may receive forgiveness of sin,
an inheritance among them which are
sanctified by faith that is in Him.

We're here to teach people about Jesus,
and show them the way to God.

We Are One

One Lord, one faith, one baptism
we're taught at one time in our lives.
As we searched for our Lord, this
worship service appeared in our lives.
As we celebrate this one year,
I wondered what has faith taught us.

And here is where I arrived:
Faith taught us to bear each
other's burdens,
For unto God, we are one.
To cry on each other's shoulders,
because we are one.
To praise our God together and
show Him that we care.
To bless God for His goodness,
to worship Him for just being God,
to thank Him for His mercies and
being ever faithful.

So what have we learned this one year
that will continue for eternity:
We've learned to lean on Jesus and
He taught us we are one.

Wanda M. Lawson

My Lord, My Love, My King

Oh Lord, you are mighty,
there is none greater than thee.
Who else could lift up their hand to heaven
and say, I live forever?
Who else could swear by Himself?
There is none greater than thee,
my Lord, my Love, my King.
You are worthy to be praised.

Who else could know me before I was formed,
and chose me anyway?
Who else could raise the sun in the east
and set it in the west?
Who else could fix the moon and the stars
perfectly in the sky?
There is none greater than thee,
my Lord, my Love, my King.

Who else could know the beginning and the end?
Who else could know all that has been told?
There is none greater than thee,
my Lord, my Love, my King.

Who else can control the wind and the waves
with just a touch of His hand?
There is none greater than thee,
my Lord, my Love, my King.

God Took Great Care When He Made You

On this day, God took His time
to make someone special,
A marvelous work, wonderfully made,
a gift from above,
God formed you with all of His love,
I believe this, I know this is true,
God took great care when He made you.

His compassion He instilled in you,
You took great care when it came to your
little one's feelings,
Careful in choosing your words so
they wouldn't be hurt.

God instilled His love inside of you,
then you spread it to all you knew,
So in watching you, your children did to.

God instilled His strength inside of you,
So in battle you would not lose,
You armed yourself with all of His armor,
No wonder the world is a brighter place.

So on this day I just want you to know,
God took great care when He made you.

Wanda M. Lawson

God Has Always Loved You

I have a message for you; it's not very long,
but listen very carefully,
God has something He wants you to know:
He has always loved you.

Before you were born He took the time
to choose the color of your eyes,
and individually numbered the hairs
on your head,
Who else would take the time to form you
and breathe life into you too?
Oh yes, God has always loved you.

Sometimes God may not like the things you do,
but He still loves you.
He takes the time to go ahead of you
to make a path that's straight and sure.
And even when you go the wrong way,
God takes the time to come and look for you.
Oh no, He will never make you come back,
but He will never give up on you.
Remember, God has always loved you.

So if by chance you're here today
and you think God has no need for you,
just ask God and you will find

*He's been trying to reach you all this time
because He's always loved you.*

Wanda M. Lawson

Lord, I Love You

Oh Lord I love You!
How much Lord, this world will never know.
If I had wings I would fly through the skies
just to let you know, Lord I love you so.

When I was in distress, You came to comfort me.
You told me to be strong and that everything would
be all right.

When I came to You for comfort,
You didn't cast me from your sight.
You watched over me by day and by night.

You took away all of my sorrows,
and carried me over all my pain.
Then You planted a new seed in me,
and in You I grew freely.
In You I grew tall and strong.
With You I can touch the sky.

Lord, You know I love you.
How much, this world will never know.
If I had wings I would fly through the heavens,
just to let You know, I love you so.

Comfort From The Lord

I was feeling hurt and was crying,
and then I heard a voice
speaking to me.

So I asked: Had you ever been
hurt or cried before?

He said: Yes, a little over
2000 years ago.

I asked: How did you get
through it?

He said: I looked at you.

Thank you Jesus

Wanda M. Lawson

My Hiding Place

The Lord is my hiding place,
He keeps me from all harm.
When the devil came to destroy me,
he couldn't pull me from the Lord's arms.

The Lord is my stronghold,
My life is in His care.
When the devil came to destroy my house,
he found the Lord there.

The devil's traps, they did not work.
His schemes, they had no power.
For every area where he tried to achieve victory,
he found the Lord is in power.

The Lord is my hiding place,
He keeps me from all harm.
When the devil tried to destroy me,
he couldn't pull me from the Lord's arms.

39 Stripes

Diseases are categorized into 39 types.
While they were beating Jesus,
He took 39 stripes.
A stripe for each category of disease.
Jesus understands.
Before you knew you were sick
Jesus had a plan in hand.
He would go to the cross to die
so we would have eternal life.
But before He would die
He would take 39 stripes.
39 stripes so we would know
all healing is in His hands.
39 stripes so sickness wouldn't
have the upper hand.
I will pray for you my sister,
my brother but you must pray too.
The disease doesn't have the upper hand
because Jesus took 39 stripes for you.

God Hasn't Forgotten You

So you have a few burdens and problems
and life is getting you down.
Know and believe God's Word is true.
God hasn't forgotten you.
He sent His Son, Jesus, to die for you.
Believe me, God is watching over you.

You may not know why or even understand
why your world is in the state that it's in.
But if you look to the hills
you will see God is there.
His arms are open wide, waiting for you.
Believe me, God hasn't forgotten you.

Take your burdens, your problems, your cares,
give them to Jesus.
But you must leave them there.
He can handle them.
Keep the faith my brother, my sister.
Believe and know God's Word is true.
God hasn't forgotten you.

God Is Wonderful

God is wonderful!
He's a wonder to behold.
He keeps His hedge of
protection around me and
constantly bless my soul.
Time after time God has kept me,
He holds me up with His
powerful right hand.
He will not let me fall.

He causes the sun to shine
to give us light and the rain
to fall to give us water.
He woke us up this morning
and He gives us food to eat.
God has never let us go hungry,
He has always provided for us.

He sends His angels to protect us,
for we are His children.
He loves us, He holds us, and He helps us.
When we stumble He picks us up.
He moves all our mountains and
opens up the sea.
Our Lord God is wonderful!
He's a wonder to behold.

Wanda M. Lawson

No More Room

In Bethlehem there came one day,
a woman named Mary,
carrying our Savior.
To the inn she and her husband went to stay.
The inn keeper came to the door and said:
"I'm sorry there is no more room."

Joseph said: "Please sir my wife
is about to deliver.
I need a place for her to rest her head."
"The stable is all I can offer",
the inn keeper said.
"For in my inn I have no more room."

So the stable Mary and Joseph did stay.
Their Jesus was born,
laid in a manger filled with hay.

So on this blessed time of year, as always,
Jesus, He will come through.
When He knocks on your door
will you let Him in or
will you tell Jesus
you have no more room.

Rest For Your Soul

You say "you're tired and weary".
This world's pressures
are getting you down.
I know a place where you can
go to find rest for your soul.
You don't have to be perfect
when you go there, but when
He's finished with you, you will be.
You can bring all your problems.
He doesn't mind a heavy load.
He's carried heavy loads before.
Come to Jesus and find
rest for your soul.

Come to Jesus!
He will make you whole.
Come to Jesus!
He will carry your load.
Come to Jesus!
He will fight all your battles.
Come to Jesus!
He will give you rest.
Come to Jesus!
He will make you whole.
Come to Jesus and find
rest for your soul.

The Wall

There was danger all around me,
turmoil on every side.
It looked like there was no escape.
I need a place to hide.

Suddenly, I was boxed in.
Walls on every side.
Everywhere I looked was closed in.
There was no where to hide.

I was in serious danger
so I called on God, My Father,
He is where I can hide.

Danger is all around the wall,
but peace is on the inside.
The danger could not come through the wall,
in fact, it didn't even try.
And the more I looked at the wall
it revealed itself from the inside.

There were no beams,
but fingers and they covered
each and every side.
The palm was beneath me,
making sure I did not fall.
The more I studied this

wall it became clear to me.
It wasn't a wall I was standing in at all,
I was standing in God's hand.

God's hand was protecting me.
It is a strong fortress that can not be moved.
When the danger saw God's hand
it swiftly began to move.

As I stood there in the midst of great peace
and joy I heard God say to me:
"I promised I would protect you and
hold you in my hand.
I gave you my peace,
I gave you my joy,
I will watch over you.
I am your hiding place,
I will fight your battles.
You are my child,
in My hands you can hide."

Wanda M. Lawson

If It Hadn't Been For The Blood

If it hadn't been for the blood,
I wouldn't have forgiveness of sin.
If it hadn't been for the blood,
I wouldn't have strength.
If it hadn't been for the blood,
I wouldn't have healing.
If it hadn't been for the blood,
I don't believe I would even be here.
If it hadn't been for the blood.

If it hadn't been for the blood,
who would have saved me from danger?
If it hadn't been for the blood,
who would have caught me when I fell.
If it hadn't been for the blood,
who would have delivered me from hell.
I'll say this and I know it's true:
"Without the blood of Jesus
we all would be doomed!"

Thanks be to God
I'll tell you I'm glad
Jesus became the Sacrificial Lamb.
Yes, Jesus, Him death could not keep.
He's coming back for His people
like a shepherd for his sheep.
Then we will gather together

at Jesus' feet.
Then He will tell us from seat to seat
how through the blood the devil met His defeat.

Wanda M. Lawson

And Then I Met God

My life was in turmoil,
I saw no change.
It was time for rearranging,
my life had to change.
I was falling and falling,
I could not stop.
I cried out for help,
and then I met God.
He saved me from this world.
He saved me from myself.
When I cried out,
He came to help.
My life needed rearranging,
my life had to change.
I was falling and falling
I could not stop.
I cried out for help,
and then I met God.

Whenever I See A Rose I Think Of Jesus

Whenever I see a rose I think of Jesus
and how sweet He is.
How He stood in the gap between God
and me so I could be set free.
Whenever I see a rose I think of Jesus
and how gentle He is.
How He carefully picks me up in His arms,
holds me and rocks me to sleep.
Whenever I see a rose I think of Jesus
and how strong He is.
The thorns are His loving arms
that keep me safe from all harm.
Whenever I see a rose I think of Jesus
because He's so bright.
Whenever you see Him He's always shining.

Wanda M. Lawson

Whenever I see a rose I think of Jesus
because He's so good to me.

Bless The Name Of The Lord!

Bless the name of the Lord!
For He is worthy!
Bless the name of the Lord!
For He protects us.
Bless the name of the Lord!
For He is great.
He sits up in heaven
controlling everything.
He sits high and looks
below at His children.
He blesses us constantly.
He enjoys our company.
He talks to us.
He listens as well.
He adores us.
No one could love us more.
Bless the name of the Lord!
I said: Bless Him!
For He is worthy.

You Say That "You Know Me"

You say that "you know Me"
and you believe that you do.
Yet not once have I ever heard
you call Me by My name.

I am the Great I AM!
Jehovah is my name.
Let me make it known to you
so you can understand.

I am Jehovah-Jireh!
The Lord God your Provider.
I will give you everything you need,
if you would just follow Me.

I am Jehovah-Sabaoth!
I am the Lord of Host!
I will command my warriors to defeat
all who come against you.
I will command the wind and
the water, the sun, the moon
and the stars to protect you.
My army will not be defeated.
I am the Lord of Host,
I keep all My promises.
I am the Commander of all,
I will never let you fall.

I am Jehovah-Nissi!
The Lord God your Banner.
Lift Me up in all your battles.
I will fight all your battles
and you will win.
There is none that can defeat Me.

I am Jehovah-Shalom!
I am your Peace.
In Me there is no torment,
only rest for your soul.

I am Jehovah-M'Kaddesh!
I am the Lord who Sanctifies.
I have set you free from all sin,
I have made you holy.
I am Jehovah-M'Kaddesh!
I have sanctified you.

I am Jehovah-Tsidkenu!
I am your Righteousness.
You were born in sin but
I made you clean.
I put My righteousness in you.

I am Jehovah-Rophe!
I am your Healer.
There is no disease I can not cure.

I am Jehovah-Gamola!
The Lord God of Recompense.
You have been faithful to Me
I will restore you.
All you have lost, all that have
slandered your name will glorify Me
because I have restored you.

I am Jehovah-Rohi!
I am your Shepherd.
You don't have to want for anything.
I am everything you need.

I am Jehovah-Shammah!
The Lord God is Present.
I am everywhere at once
and always with you.

I am Elohim!
Your Creator, and Loving Father!
I created you, made you and
I know all your thoughts.

I am El Shaddi!
The God that's more than enough.
When a problem comes your way
and it seems too hard for you,
give it to Me,

I am more than enough too
handle it for you.

I am El Elyon!
The God Most High.
There is nothing higher than I.
There is no problem, no sickness,
no circumstance, nothing higher
than Me.

The angels bow before Me,
the fields clap their hands,
elements obey Me and
I command the universe.

Some call Me Father God,
still others call Me Lord.
Some call Me in the morning
others call Me late at night.

You say that "you know Me,"
and I know you believe you do.
Then if you really know Me,
My name you should use.
You say that, "you know Me,"
then call Me by My name.

Wanda M. Lawson

I AM

I am beautiful
I am persecuted
I am an overcomer
I am strong
I am victorious
I am a child of God

I am in a battle
I am in God's army
I am a winner
I am prosperous
I am redeemed
I am a joint heir
with Jesus Christ

I am wonderfully made
I am full of joy
I am more precious
than any jewel
I am flying with
wings of eagles
I am a conqueror
I am covered by the blood

I am not the Great I AM
but I am His
I am covered by the blood

I am a joint heir
with Jesus Christ
I am a child of God
and I belong to Him

Wanda M. Lawson

Bless My Soul I Met The Lord
And He Took Me In

I was tired and weary, about to give up hope.
I had taken a handful of pills,
I was going to give up the ghost.
Before I laid down for what I thought
would be my final sleep,
I prayed to God to ease my pain
and for my soul to keep.
And wouldn't you know bless my soul
I met the Lord and He took me in.

I woke up the next morning,
much to my surprise,
God heard my cry.
Why didn't He let me die?
Then I heard a voice
which came from above:
Your job my child,
you have not done.
I could not let you turn
coward and run.
Your job, it is not done.

What job could I possibly do?
I am only human.

Through your words I will bless
souls and then I will take them in.

What's so special about me?
I'm not the prettiest one.
I stutter,
I can't always find the right words.
I even get nervous when
in front of a crowd.

But you did the one thing
most people never do.
You prayed for My help which
is all anyone needs to do.
And then on the paper
you began to tell everyone
the things I told you.

It's hard for people to hear me now
but all my children do.
I want to give you this
message for all the world to see.

Before you go out in this world
or tackle your daily trials,
pray to God to give you strength
and for your soul to keep.
And wouldn't you know
bless your soul you will meet the
Lord and He will take you in.

Wanda M. Lawson

Never Say You're Sick

Never say you're sick!
You're a child of God.
Do not say "I'm sick."
By His stripes you are healed.
Never contradict God's word.
It shows you don't
fully trust Him.
Never say you're sick!
You are being healed.
Accept your healing
and trust in God.

God Is Better Than Gold

God is better than gold
His wisdom more precious
than fine silver
He cause kings to reign
His judgment rules
He has the final say

All the riches are His
The wisdom is His

His children rise when
they follow His direction
They fall when they do not
Yet He catches them
for they are His

He provides clothes
with no thread
Food with no seed
and water with no rain

All that are wise fear Him
for He is God
He has the power to stop all
yet He shows mercy
He has the cure for all disease
All knowledge is in His hands

Wanda M. Lawson

To obey Him is eternal life
To know Him is to know wisdom
God is better than gold
His wisdom more precious
than fine silver

All scripture is inspired by God.

I find that it inspires poetry as well.

Wanda M. Lawson

Section II

The Scriptures

Wanda M. Lawson

Look At What We've Done
To What God Gave Us

"Be angry, and do not sin":
do not let the sun
go down on your wrath.

Ephesians 4:26

Wanda M. Lawson

<u>Untitled</u>

Judge not, that you be not judged.

Matthew 7:1

...Unto The Lord

I will sing to the Lord
as long as I live:
I will sing praise to my God
while I have my being.

Psalm 104:33

And now my head shall be lifted
up above my enemies all around me;
therefore I will offer sacrifices of
joy in His tabernacle;
I will sing, yes, I will sing praises
to the Lord.

Psalm 27:6

I acknowledged my sin to You,
and my iniquity I have not hidden.
I said, "I will confess my
transgressions to the Lord,"
and You forgave the iniquity of my sin.

Psalm 32:5

It is good to give thanks to the Lord,
and to sing praises to Your name,
O Most High

Psalm 92:1

Oh, sing to the Lord a new song!
Sing to the Lord, all the earth.
Sing to the Lord, bless His name;
proclaim the good news of His
salvation from day to day.

Psalm 96:1-2

Oh, sing to the Lord a new song!
For He has done marvelous things;
His right hand and His holy arm
have gained Him the victory.

Psalm 98:1

I will pay my vows to the Lord
now in the presence of all His people.

Psalm 116:14

<u>Come Unto Me</u>

"*Come to Me, all you who labor
and are heavy laden, and
I will give you rest.*"

Matthew 11:28

"*Most assuredly, I say to you,
he who hears My word and
believes in Him who sent Me
has everlasting life, and shall
not come into judgement, but has
passed from death into life.*"

John 5:24

Wanda M. Lawson

How Precious I Must Be

"I have been crucified with Christ;
it is no longer I who live,
but Christ lives in me; and
the life which I now live in
the flesh I live by faith in
the Son of God, who loved
me and gave Himself for me."

Galatians 2:20

Children Of The Living God

We are hard pressed on every side,
yet not crushed; we are perplexed,
but not in despair, persecuted,
but not forsaken; struck down
but not destroyed

2 Corinthians 4:8-9

Wanda M. Lawson

<u>How I Love Thee</u>

"See I have set before you today
life and good, death and evil,
in that I command you today
to love the Lord your God,
to walk in His ways, and to
keep His commandments,
His statutes, and His judgments,
that you may live and multiply;
and the Lord your God will bless
you in the land which you go to possess."

Deuteronomy 30:15-16

"Teacher, which is the great
commandment in the law?"
Jesus said to him,
"You shall love the Lord your God
with all your heart, with all your
soul, and with all your mind."

Matthew 22:36-37

<u>*Why Are We Here?*</u>

"To open their eyes and to turn
them from darkness to light, and from
the power of Satan to God, that
they may receive forgiveness of sins
and an inheritance among those who
are sanctified by faith in Me."

Acts 26:18

We Are One

"As You sent Me into the world,
I also have sent them into the world.
And for their sakes I sanctify Myself,
that they also may be sanctified by
the truth. I do not pray for these alone,
but also for those who will believe in
Me through their word; that they all
may be one, as You, Father, are in Me,
and I in You; that they also may be one
in Us, that the world may believe that
You sent Me. And the glory which
You gave Me I have given them,
that they may be one just as
We are one"

John 17:18-22

My Lord, My Love, My King

By Myself I have sworn, says the Lord,
because you have done this thing,
and have not withheld your son,
your only son blessings I will bless you
and multiplying I will multiply your
descendants as the stars of the heaven
and as the sand which is on the seashore;
and your descendants shall possess the
gate of their enemies.

Genesis 22:16-17

For I raise My hand to heaven,
and say, "As I live forever"

Deuteronomy 32:40

For when God made a promise to Abraham,
because He could swear by no one greater,
He swore by Himself, saying, "Surely blessing
I will bless you, and multiplying I will
multiply you. And so, after he had patiently
endured, he obtained the promise.

Hebrews 6:13-15

> *And there shall be no more curse,*
> *but the throne of God and of the*
> *Lamb shall be in it, and His servants*
> *shall serve Him.*
>
> *Revelations 22:3*

God Took Great Care When He Made You

Then God said, "Let Us make man
in Our image, according to Our likeness;
let them have dominion over the fish of
the sea, over the birds of the air, and over
the cattle, over all the earth and over every
creeping thing that creeps over the earth."

Genesis 1:26

I will praise You, for I am
fearfully and wonderfully made;
marvelous are Your works
and that my soul knows very well.

Psalm 139:14

Put on the whole armor of God,
that you may be able to stand
against the wiles of the devil.
For we do not wrestle against
flesh and blood, but against
principalities, against powers,
against the rulers of the darkness
of this age, against spiritual hosts
of wickedness in the heavenly
places. Therefore take up the
whole armor of God, that you

*may be able to withstand in the
evil day, and having done all, to
stand. Stand therefore, having
girded your waist with truth,
having put on the breastplate
of righteousness, and having
shod your feet with the preparation
of the gospel of peace; above all
taking the shield of faith with
which you will be able to quench
all the fiery darts of the wicked one.
And take the hamlet of salvation,
and the sword of the Spirit, which
is the word of God*

Ephesians 6:11-17

<u>God Has Always Loved You</u>

*And the Lord God formed man
of the dust of the ground, and
breathed into his nostrils the
breath of life; and man became
a living being.*

Genesis 2:7

*And the Lord God caused a
deep sleep to fall on Adam,
and he slept; and He took one
of his ribs, and closed up the
flesh in its place. Then the rib
which the Lord God had taken
from man He made into a woman,
and He brought her to the man.*

Genesis 2:21-22

*But the very hairs of your head
are all numbered.*

Matthew 10:30

*Then one of the criminals who were
hanged blasphemed Him, saying,
"If You are the Christ, save Yourself*

and us." But the other, answering,
"Do you not even fear God, seeing
you are under the same condemnation?
And we indeed justly, for we receive
the due reward of our deeds; but this
Man has done nothing wrong."
Then he said to Jesus, "Lord, remember
me when You come into Your kingdom."
And Jesus said to him, "Assuredly, I say
to you, today you will be with Me in Paradise."

Luke 23:39-42

Lord, I Love You

*In my distress I called upon
the Lord, and cried out to
my God; He heard my voice
from His temple, and my cry
entered His ears.*

2 Samuel 22:7

*Hear me when I call, O God
of my righteousness!
You have relieved me in my
distress; Have mercy on me,
and hear my prayer.*

Psalm 4:1

*I called on the Lord in distress;
The Lord answered me and set
me in a broad place.*

Psalm 118:5

*In my distress I cried to
the Lord and He heard me.*

Psalm 120:1

Comfort From The Lord

"Sanctify them by Your truth.
Your word is truth. As You
sent Me into the world,
I also have sent them into
the world. And for their
sakes I sanctify Myself, that
they also may be sanctified
by the truth."

John 19:17-19

...saying, "Father, if it is
Your will, take this cup
away from Me; nevertheless
not My will, but Yours, be done."
Then an angel appeared to Him
from heaven, strengthening Him.
And being in agony, He prayed
more earnestly. Then His sweat
became like great drops of blood
falling down to the ground.

Luke 22:42-44

My Hiding Place

For in the time of trouble
He shall hide me in His
pavilion; In the secret
place of His tabernacle
He shall hide me; He shall
set me high upon a rock.

Psalm 27:5

<u>39 Stripes</u>

*Surely He has borne our griefs
and carried our sorrows;
yet we esteemed Him stricken,
smitten by God, and afflicted.
But He was wounded for our
transgressions, He was bruised
for our iniquities;
the chastisement for our peace
was upon Him,
and by His stripes we are healed.*

Isaiah 53:4-5

*But God demonstrates His own
love towards us, in that while
we were still sinners, Christ
died for us.*

Romans 5:8

God Hasn't Forgotten You

"Are not five sparrows sold
for two copper coins?
And not one of them is
forgotten before God.
But the very hairs of
your head are all numbered.
Do not fear therefore;
you are of more value
than many sparrows."

Luke 12:6-7

<u>God Is Wonderful</u>

Many, O Lord my God,
are Your wonderful works
which You have done;
And Your thoughts toward
us cannot be recounted to
You in order; If I would
declare and speak of them,
they are more than can
be numbered.

Psalm 40:5

O Lord, You are my God.
I will exalt You,
I will praise Your name,
For You have done wonderful
things; Your counsels of old
are faithfulness and truth.

Isaiah 25:1

No More Room

*And she brought forth her
firstborn Son, and wrapped
Him in swaddling clothes,
and laid Him in a manger,
because there was no room
for them in the inn.*

Luke 2:7

*And Jesus said to him,
"Foxes have holes and
birds of the air have nests,
but the Son of Man has
nowhere to lay His head.*

Matthew 8:20

<u>Rest For Your Soul</u>

*Take My yoke upon you and
learn from Me, for I am gentle
and lowly in heart, and you will
find rest for your soul.*

Matthew 11:29

The Wall

"And I give them eternal life,
and they shall never perish;
neither shall anyone snatch them
out of My hand. My Father,
who has given them to Me, is
greater than all; and no one is
able to snatch them out of My
Father's hand.
I and My Father are one."

John 10:28-30

Wanda M. Lawson

<u>*If It Hadn't Been For The Blood*</u>

*But God demonstrates His own love
toward us, in that while we were
yet sinners, Christ died for us.
Much more then, having not been
justified by His blood, we shall
be saved from wrath through Him.*

Romans 5:8-9

And Then I Met God

For You have delivered my soul
from death.
Have You not kept my feet from falling,
that I may walk before God
in the light of the living?

Psalm 56:13

Wanda M. Lawson

<u>Whenever I See A Rose I Think Of Jesus</u>

*I am the Rose Of Sharon
and the Lily of the Valleys.*

Song of Solomon 2:1

Bless The Name Of The Lord

*Sing to the Lord, bless
His name; Proclaim the
good news of His
salvation from day to day.*

Psalm 96:2

*Bless the Lord, O my soul;
and all that is within me,
bless His holy name!
Bless the Lord, O my soul
and forget not all His benefits*

Psalm 103:1-2

*My mouth shall speak the
praise of the Lord, and all
flesh shall bless His holy
name forever and ever.*

Psalm 145:21

<u>*You Say That "You Know Me"*</u>

*Then Moses said to God,
"Indeed, when I come to
the children of Israel and
say to them, 'The God of
your fathers has sent me
to you,' and they say to me,
'What is His name?'
What shall I say to them?"
And God said to Moses,
"I AM WHO I AM"
And He said, "Thus you
shall say to the children of
Israel, 'I AM has sent me
to you.'"*

Exodus 3:13-14

<u>*Jehovah-Jireh*</u>

*...And Abraham called the name of
the place, The-Lord-Will-Provide;
as it is said to the day, "In the Mount
of the Lord it shall be provided."*

Genesis 22:14

Jehovah-Sabaoth

*"Like birds flying about,
so will the Lord of Host defend
Jerusalem. Defending He will
also deliver it; passing over,
He will preserve it."*

Isaiah 31:5

Jehovah-Nissi

*But Moses' hands became heavy;
so they took a stone and put it
under him, and he sat on it. And
Aaron and Hur supported his hands,
one on one side, and the other on the
other side; and his hands were steady
until the going down of the sun.
And Moses built an alter and called
its name, The-Lord-Is-My-Banner.*

Exodus 17:12,15

Jehovah-Shalom

*Then the Lord said to him,
"Peace be with you; do not fear,
you will not die." So Gideon
built an alter there to the Lord,*

and called it The-Lord-Is-Peace.
To this day it is still in Ophrah
of the Abiezrites.

Judges 6:23-24

Jehovah-M'Kaddesh

"Speak also to the children of Israel,
saying, 'Surely My Sabbaths you shall
keep, for it is a sign between Me and
You throughout your generations, that
you may know that I am the Lord who
sanctifies you.'"

Exodus 31:13

Jehovah-Tsidkenu

"Behold, the days are coming,"
says the Lord,
"That I will raise to David a Branch
of righteousness; A King shall reign
and prosper, and execute judgment
and righteousness in the earth.
In His days Judah will be saved,
and Israel will dwell safely; Now this

is the name by which He will be called:
THE LORD OUR RIGHTEOUSNESS."

Jeremiah 23:5-6

Jehovah-Rophe

... "If you diligently heed the voice
of the Lord your God and do what is
right in His sight, give ear to His
commandments and keep all His statutes,
I will put none of these diseases on you
which I have brought on the Egyptians.
For I am the Lord who heals you.

Exodus 15:26

Jehovah-Gamola

Because the plunderer comes
against her, against Babylon,
and her mighty men are taken.
Every one of their bows is broken;
for the Lord is the God of Recompense,
He will surely repay.

Jeremiah 51:56

Jehovah-Rohi

The Lord is my shepherd;
I shall not want.
He makes me to lie down in
green pastures;
He leads me beside the still waters.
He restores my soul;
He leads me in the paths of
righteousness for His name sake.

Psalm 23:1-2

Jehovah-Shammah

"All the way around shall be
eighteen thousand cubits;
and the name of the city from
that day shall be:
THE LORD IS THERE."

Ezekiel 48:35

Elohim

This is the history of the heavens
and the earth when they were
created, in the day that the Lord God
made the earth and the heavens,
before any plant of the field was in

the earth and before any herb of the
field had grown. For the Lord God
had not caused it to rain on the earth,
and there was no man to till the ground;
but a mist went up from the earth and
watered the whole face of the ground.
And the Lord God formed man of the
dust of the ground, and breathed into
his nostrils the breath of life; and
man became a living being.

Genesis 2:4-7

El Shaddi

When Abram was ninety-nine
years old the Lord appeared to
Abram and said to him, "I am
Almighty God; walk before Me
and be blameless. And I will make
My covenant between Me and you
and will multiply you exceedingly."
Then Abram fell on his face, and God
talked with him, saying: "As for Me,
behold, My covenant is with you,
and you shall be a father of many
nations. No longer shall your name
be called Abram, but your name shall

be Abraham; for I have made you a
father of many nations."

Genesis 17:1-5

<u>El Elyon</u>

…"Blessed be Abram of God Most High,
Possessor of heaven and earth:
and blessed by God Most High,
who had delivered your enemies into
your hand."
And he gave him a tithe of all.

Genesis 14:19-20

I AM

*Blessed are those who are persecuted
for righteousness' sake, for theirs
is the kingdom of heaven. Blessed are
you when they revile and persecuted
you, and say all kinds of evil against
you falsely for My sake. Rejoice and
be exceedingly glad, for great is your
reward in heaven, for so they persecuted
the prophets who were before you.*

Matthew 5:10-12

*The Spirit Himself bears witness with
our spirit that we are children of God,
and if children, then heirs – heirs of God
and joint heirs with Christ, if indeed
we suffer with Him, that we may also
be glorified together.*

Romans 8:16-17

For whatever is born of God overcomes
the world. And this is the victory that
has overcome the world – our faith.

1 John 5:4

Christ had redeemed us from the curse of
the law, having become a curse for us
(for it is written, "Cursed is everyone
who hangs on a tree")

Galatians 3:13

I will praise You, for I am fearfully
and wonderfully made;
marvelous are Your works,
and that my soul knows very well.

Psalm 139:14

But those who wait on the Lord
shall renew their strength;
they shall mount up with wings
like eagles,
they shall run and not be weary,
they shall walk and not faint.

Isaiah 40:31

Not with the blood of goats and
calves, but with His own blood
He entered the Most Holy Place
once for all, having obtained
eternal redemption.
How much more shall the blood
of Christ, who through the eternal
Spirit offered Himself without spot
to God, cleanse your conscience from
dead works to serve the living God?
And for this reason He is the Mediator
of the new covenant, by means of death,
for the redemption of the
transgressions under the first covenant,
that those who are called may receive
the promise of the eternal inheritance.

Hebrews 9:12, 14-15

Wanda M. Lawson

Bless My Soul I Met The Lord And He Took Me In

"For this is the covenant that I will
make with the house of Israel after those
days, says the Lord: I will put My
laws in their mind and write them
on their hearts; and I will be their
God, and they shall be My people.
None of them shall teach his neighbor,
and none his brother, saying 'Know
the Lord,' for all shall know Me,
from the least of them to the greatest
of them. For I will be merciful to
their unrighteousness, and their
sins and their lawless deeds I will
remember no more."

Hebrews 8:10-12

<u>Never Say You're Sick</u>

*Surely He has borne our griefs
and carried our sorrows;
yet we esteemed Him stricken,
smitten by God, and afflicted.
But He was wounded for our
transgressions, He was bruised
for our iniquities;
the chastisement for our peace
was upon Him,
and by His stripes we are healed.*

Isaiah 53:4-5

Wanda M. Lawson

<u>God Is Better Than Gold</u>

*The law of Your mouth is better
to me then thousands of coins
of gold and silver.*

Psalm 119:72

*How much better to get wisdom
than gold! And to get understanding
is to be chosen rather than silver.*

Proverbs 16:16

*"The silver is Mine, and the gold is Mine,"
says the Lord of Host.*

Haggai 2:8

About the Author

I was born March 16, 1965 in Washington, DC. I grew up in Northwest DC and Shenandoah, Virginia. In 1980 I moved back to Washington, DC.

In 1991, I join the Emmanuel Baptist Church where I am still a current disciple. At Emmanuel I sing in the choir, attend Sunday school, bible study and I am an advisor for the step team.

My life at Emmanuel has helped me to grow closer to God. The things my pastor, Dr. Clinton W. Austin, has taught through God's Word will stay with me all of my days.

As a member of Children of the Living God, a prayer and bible study group, I have learned to find myself in Christ and that He can use anyone.

In 1997, I graduated from Southeastern University with an Associates Degree in Computer Information Systems. At Southeastern University I became a member of Phi Chi Theta Fraternity of Business and Economics, Inc. and Delta Sigma Theta Sorority Inc.

Now I'm pursuing an Associates Degree in Business Management at Northern Virginia Community College (NOVA), after which I will pursue my Bachelors Degree in

Business Management. I haven't decided on a college for my Bachelors Degree just yet. I'm waiting on a word from God on where to go.

About this Awesome Gift from God

"Come Unto Me" was my first published work. It was published in the anthology "On Summers Passing" by the National Library of Poetry. My poem "Children of the Living God" was published in the anthology "Outstanding Poets of 1998.The third "My Hiding Place" was published in the anthology "America at the Millennium: The Best Poems and Poets of the 20th Century".This was a great honor to me.

As a child of God I have learned the following lessons:
Trust in God in everything you do.
Let God lead your life.
Before you make a discussion, ask God and...wait for the answer.

www.ingramcontent.com/pod-product-compliance
Lightning Source LLC
Chambersburg PA
CBHW030354290526
45785CB00004B/1741